THE AWAKENED SOUL'S FIELD MANUAL

THE AWAKENED SOUL'S FIELD MANUAL

A Practical Guide to Living Consciously

Nicole I. Burgess

Copyright © 2025 by Nicole I. Burgess

All rights reserved. No part of this book may be reproduced, distributed, or transmitted in any form or by any means, including photocopying, recording, or other electronic or mechanical methods, without the prior written permission of the publisher, except in the case of brief quotations embodied in critical reviews and certain other noncommercial uses permitted by copyright law.

Published by NBM Publishing, LLC Chapel Hill, North Carolina
ISBN: 9798994453940
First Edition, 2025

The information and practices in this book are based on the author's personal experience and research. They are not intended to replace professional medical, psychological, or legal advice. Readers are encouraged to consult qualified professionals for specific health concerns and to use their own discernment when applying any spiritual practices.

Disclaimer: The views and practices expressed in this book reflect ancient wisdom traditions and the author's personal spiritual journey. Individual results and experiences may vary. The author and publisher assume no responsibility for actions taken by readers based on the information presented herein.

For more information about the author and her work:
www.nbmbooks.com

Printed in the United States of America

Cover design by Nicole I. Burgess

TABLE OF CONTENTS

PART ONE: WELCOME HOME

Introduction: You're Not Alone **1**

What Does It Mean to Be Awakened? **4**

The Journey Ahead: Foundation & Mastery **7**

Reading This Guide **10**

PART TWO: FOUNDATION PRACTICES

Practice 1: Sacred Wisdom & Ancient Texts **15**

Practice 2: Earth Connection – Stand on Dirt **18**

Practice 3: Sound Healing & Frequency **21**

Practice 4: Nourishing the Temple **24**

Practice 5: Detoxification Practices **27**

Practice 6: Conscious Community **30**

Practice 7: Celestial Awareness **33**

Practice 8: Listening to Earth's Messengers **36**

Practice 9: Grow a Garden **39**

Practice 10: The Temporary Nature of Physical Reality **42**

INTERLUDE: CHECKPOINT

Before You Continue: A Note on Advanced Practices **46**

Self-Assessment Questions **50**

My Awakening Journey So Far **53**

PART THREE: MASTERY PRACTICES

Practice 11: Eliminating Fear **60**

Practice 12: The Power of Words **63**

Affirmations **66**

Practice 13: Meditative Action & Psychic Development **70**

Signs You're on The Path **73**

Practice 14: Dream Mastery & Astral Work **75**

Practice 15: Understanding Imbalance vs. Illness **80**

Practice 16: Natural Fibers & Energetic Harmony **85**

Practice 17: Biodynamic Gardening **88**

Practice 18: Sacred Hair Practices **91**

Practice 19: Lunar Cycle Syncing (For Women) **94**

Practice 20: Visualization & Manifestation **97**

Practice 21: Karma – Cause & Effect **100**

Practice 22: Sacred Languages **103**

Practice 23: Astrological Wisdom in Ancient Texts **108**

Practice 24: Discipline & Integrity **113**

Practice 25: You Are the Creator **116**

PART FOUR: INTEGRATION

Living as an Awakened Being **122**

When You Forget (And You Will) **126**

Emergency Grounding Techniques **129**

Resources & Further Study **132**

My Commitment to Consciousness **135**

Glossary **138**

About the Author **149**

HOW TO USE THIS BOOK

This is not a book to read once and shelve. This is a field manual, a companion and a mirror. You'll return to it again and again as you navigate the strange and beautiful terrain of awakened consciousness.

If you're newly awakened, start with Part Two. The Foundation Practices are your anchor. Don't rush through them. Some will feel natural immediately; others might take months or years to integrate. That's exactly as it should be.

If you've been walking this path for seven years or more, you may be ready for Part Three. But here's the truth: mastery isn't linear. You might need to return to the foundations even as you explore advanced practices. There's no shame in beginning again. The spiral path means we revisit the same lessons at deeper levels.

About the journaling spaces: They're small by design. You're not writing essays here, you're planting seeds. A single sentence can hold an entire revelation. Date your entries. You'll be amazed when you return to see how far you've traveled.

A word of caution: Some of what you read here will sound impossible. You might think, "I could never do that," or "That's too far." Trust yourself. Take what resonates, leave what doesn't, and come back when you're ready. The universe has infinite patience, and so should you.

This book won't awaken you, you've already done that. This book simply reminds you that you're not alone, you're not crazy, and yes, there is a path forward.

Welcome home.

PART ONE: WELCOME HOME

Introduction: You're Not Alone

You woke up.

Maybe it happened suddenly, you had a moment of clarity so profound it shattered everything you thought you knew. Or maybe it crept in slowly. That gnawing feeling. A growing discomfort with the script you'd been handed, the life you were told to want. Either way, you're here now, awake in a world that still seems to be sleeping.

And it's lonely, isn't it?

The people around you are talking about things that suddenly feel hollow. Discussing weekend plans, television shows, and the endless accumulation of things that don't matter. You try to engage, but there's a distance now, a gap between their reality and yours. You wonder if you're going crazy, you wonder if you're the only one who sees through the illusion.

Let me tell you something true: **You are not alone.**

Across the earth plane, souls are waking up. Some of them are your neighbors, some are on the other side of the world. They're feeling exactly what you're feeling - confusion, isolation, and the desperate need for something *real*. They're searching for purpose, for meaning, for a way to live that honors what they now know to be true.

You are part of an ancient lineage of awakened beings. The mystics, the seers and the wise ones who came before you walked this same path. They felt this same loneliness. And they left breadcrumbs for you to follow.

This book is one of those breadcrumbs.

I won't pretend the path ahead is easy. Awakening isn't a destination, it's a practice, a way of being. It's a daily choice to see clearly in a world that profits from your blindness. You'll stumble. You'll doubt. You'll have days when you want to go back to sleep because sleep was so much simpler.

But here's what I know: you can't unknow what you know. You can't unsee what's been shown to you. The door you walked through doesn't open backwards. And on the other side of the loneliness, on the other side of the fear, there is something magnificent waiting for you.

Connection. Purpose. Peace.

A life aligned with the truth of who you really are.

So, take a moment and breathe. You're exactly where you're meant to be. And you're not walking alone.

What Does It Mean to Be Awakened?

Awakening is remembering.

Simple as that. It's not learning something new, but recalling the ancient memory that is true for all beings: you are not separate from the universe. You are not an isolated fragment stumbling through a random existence. You are an expression of the Great Spirit, the universal source energy, having a temporary human experience.

You are the ocean pretending to be a wave. You are the universe looking at itself through your eyes.

Awakening is the moment you stop pretending.

It's when you recognize that the rules you were taught, which are to work hard, buy things, compete, fear death, are just stories. Useful stories perhaps, for keeping society running, but not ultimate truths. Not *the* truth.

When you awaken, you begin to see the machinery behind the curtain, the reality behind the illusion, the truth behind the maya. You notice how fear is used to control. How distraction keeps people numb. How the pace of modern life is designed to prevent the very stillness that leads to awakening.

But awakening isn't just about seeing what's false. It's about remembering what's true:

- That everything is energy, and you are part of that eternal flow
- That your thoughts create your reality more powerfully than your actions
- That time is not linear, and death is not an ending
- That you are loved beyond measure, held by a benevolent universe
- That your purpose is not to acquire or achieve, but to remember and express your divine nature

This knowing changes everything.

Suddenly, you can't participate in the old games with the same enthusiasm. Small talk feels suffocating. Materialism feels empty. The rat race reveals itself as exactly that, a race with no finish line and no prize truly worth having.

You become hungry for authenticity and depth, for teaching and practices that actually nourish your soul instead of numbing it.

This hunger is good and this restlessness is sacred. It means you're ready.

The Journey Ahead: Foundation & Mastery

The path of the awakened soul unfolds in layers, like a flower opening to the sun.

Foundation (Tips 1-10) is about grounding yourself in new practices. These are the daily disciplines that anchor your awakening in the physical world. You'll learn to reconnect with the earth, purify your vessel, simplify your life, and attune to the natural rhythms that society has taught you to ignore.

Foundation work is not glamorous. It's dirt under your fingernails and vegetables on your plate. It's standing outside barefoot even when your neighbors think you're strange. It's choosing silence over noise, quality over quantity, depth over distraction.

Do not rush through foundation. Some people spend their entire lives here, and that's perfectly fine. A strong foundation is everything. Without it, the advanced practices become destabilizing and even dangerous.

Mastery (Tips 11-25) is for those who have walked the path for at least seven years, ideally fourteen to twenty-one. These practices require a level of energetic stability, self-knowledge, and discipline that can only be earned through time and dedication.

In mastery, you'll work with fear elimination, reality creation, dream control, and consciousness expansion. You'll learn to read the hidden meanings in sacred texts, sync your body with celestial rhythms, and take full responsibility as the creator of your experience.

This is not spiritual bypassing. This is not pretending you've transcended your humanity. This is the deep, often uncomfortable work of integrating your divine nature with your human existence.

How do you know when you're ready to move from foundation to mastery?

You'll know. Your foundation practices will feel effortless and automatic. You'll have healed your major wounds. You'll have cultivated genuine self-discipline. And most importantly, you'll feel called forward, not from ego's desire to be "advanced," but from soul's readiness to expand.

Trust the timing because the universe has no deadlines.

READING THIS GUIDE

This book is structured for practical use:

Each practice includes:

- The specific steps (what to actually do)
- The why behind it (understanding deepens commitment)
- A journal prompt (for integration and reflection)
- Space to write (because insight without recording is often insight forgotten)

Some suggestions as you work with this material:

Take your time. One practice per week, or even per month, is perfectly appropriate. Depth matters more than speed.

Personalize it. If a practice doesn't resonate with you, modify it. Your intuition is valid. The universe speaks to you directly therefore you don't need my permission to adapt these teachings.

Be gentle with yourself because you will forget. You will slip back into old patterns. You will have days when you feel completely uprooted from your awakened knowing. This is a normal part of the process. Compassion for your humanity is itself a spiritual practice.

Journal consistently and date your entries. In six months, or six years, you'll want to see how far you've come.

Find your people. This path is walked alone, but it doesn't have to be walked in isolation. Seek out others who understand. Build authentic community, even if it's small.

And finally: **Trust yourself.** You picked up this book because something in you recognized it. That same inner knowing will guide you through every practice, every challenge, and every moment of doubt.

You have everything you need already inside you.

Now let's begin.

PART TWO: FOUNDATION PRACTICES

For the newly awakened soul

Practice 1: Sacred Wisdom & Ancient Texts

THE PRACTICE:

Read the sacred texts from every ancient culture you can access. Not as religious doctrine, but as wisdom literature. The Bhagavad Gita, the Tao Te Ching, the Bible, the Quran, the Mahabharata, the Upanishads, Norse Eddas, the Enuma Elish, indigenous oral traditions that have been transcribed, all of them.

Start your morning or end your evening with even fifteen minutes of reading. Let the words wash over you. Notice what resonates. Notice what doesn't. Keep a running list of texts you want to explore.

WHY IT MATTERS:

These texts are maps left by those who walked the path before you. They speak in metaphor and symbol, pointing toward truths that can't be captured in plain language. When you read them with awakened eyes, you'll begin to see the common thread running through all traditions - the same universal wisdom expressed in different cultural languages. You're not looking for rules to follow. You're looking for resonance, for recognition, for the feeling of "yes, I remember this".

JOURNAL PROMPT:

What sacred text called to me today? What single line or image stayed with me?

JOURNALING SPACE:

_____

_____

_____

_____

_____

Practice 2: Earth Connection - Stand on Dirt

THE PRACTICE:

Every single day, put your bare feet on the earth. Grass, soil, sand, stone, it doesn't matter. Just make direct contact between your skin and the ground. Five minutes minimum. Longer if you can.

No shoes. No socks. No barrier between you and the earth.

Stand there and breathe. Feel the energy exchange. Let the earth absorb what you no longer need. Let it tell you what you do.

WHY IT MATTERS:

You are an electrical being living on an electromagnetic earth. Modern life has insulated you with rubber soles, concrete floors, and high-rise apartments. This disconnection is not neutral. It disrupts your natural bioelectrical field and leaves you frazzled, anxious, and ungrounded. The earth is literally designed to recalibrate you. This isn't metaphor, it's physics. The ground beneath you carries a negative charge that neutralizes the free radicals building up in your body from stress, electronics, and inflammation. Five minutes of bare feet on earth ("earthing" or "grounding") can measurably reduce cortisol and improve sleep. But more than that, you'll feel it. That sense of coming home to your body, of connecting to the earth and the world around you, that's real.

JOURNAL PROMPT:

How did my body feel before and after connecting with the earth today?

JOURNALING SPACE:

_____

_____

_____

Practice 3: Sound Healing & Frequency

THE PRACTICE:

Recalibrate your energy field daily with intentional sound. Choose from: binaural beats, Gregorian chanting, singing bowls, chimes, recorded ocean sounds, and bells.

Create a morning or evening ritual. Even ten minutes. Put on headphones or let the sound fill your space. Close your eyes. Let the frequencies move through you. Don't just hear it, feel it in your chest, your bones, and your cells.

Experiment with different sounds on different days. Notice what your system feels drawn towards.

WHY IT MATTERS:

Everything is vibration. Your body, your thoughts, your emotions, all of it is frequency. When you've been swimming in the chaotic frequencies of modern life (traffic, arguments, bad news, light pollution, electromagnetic radiation), your field gets scrambled. Sound healing isn't entertainment, it's focused recalibration. Certain frequencies have been used for thousands of years because they work - they bring your system back into coherence and harmony. Gregorian chants were designed to induce altered states. Tibetan bowls create overtones that synchronize brainwaves. Ocean sounds remind your nervous system of the womb. You're not just relaxing. You're tuning your instrument.

JOURNAL PROMPT:

What did I notice in my body or mind during today's sound practice?

JOURNALING SPACE:

_____

_____

_____

Practice 4: Nourishing the Temple

THE PRACTICE:

Eat whole foods, with particular attention to dark green leafy vegetables and purple or black fruits.

This means: spinach, kale, collards, chard; blueberries, blackberries, blackcurrants, plums, black grapes, elderberries, dates, figs, acai berries, purple carrots, purple cabbage, and eggplant.

If it comes in a box with a list of ingredients you can't pronounce, it's not whole food. If it grew from the earth or came from an animal that ate what grew from the earth, it probably is.

Simple as that.

WHY IT MATTERS:

Your body is not separate from your spiritual practice, it's the vehicle for it. You cannot do deep consciousness work in a toxic, depleted vessel. Dark leafy greens are the most nutrient-dense foods on earth, packed with chlorophyll (liquid sunlight), minerals, and life force. Purple and black fruits are rich in anthocyanins, powerful antioxidants that protect your cells and brain. These foods literally raise your vibration. They make you clearer, lighter, more receptive. When you eat processed food, you're consuming dead things that have been stripped of life force and pumped full of chemicals. When you eat living food, you're consuming light. You become what you eat. Choose accordingly.

JOURNAL PROMPT:

What living foods did I nourish myself with today? How did they make me feel?

JOURNALING SPACE:

_____

_____

_____

_____

Practice 5: Detoxification Practices

THE PRACTICE:

Support your body's natural detoxification with these tools: spirulina, chlorella, sea moss, liquid chlorophyll, MSM, and food-grade diatomaceous earth.

Start with one or two. Research proper dosing and listen to your body. These are not quick fixes; they're ongoing support for a system constantly bombarded by toxins.

Rotate them, give your body breaks, and stay hydrated.

WHY IT MATTERS:

You're living in a toxic world. That's not spiritual bypassing, it's just fact. Heavy metals in the water, pesticides in the food, chemicals in the air, plastics everywhere, radiofrequencies and electromagnetic fields constantly. Your body is working overtime to process all of this. These detoxifiers help. Spirulina and chlorella bind to heavy metals and escort them out; sea moss provides the essential trace minerals your body needs; chlorophyll oxygenates and alkalizes, it also neutralizes acidity and balances the internal pH; MSM supports cellular detox and repair; and diatomaceous earth gently scrubs the digestive tract. When your physical body is cleaner, your energetic body becomes clearer. You'll sleep better, think sharper, and feel lighter. Detox is not a trend, it's a necessity for anyone doing consciousness work in the 21st century.

JOURNAL PROMPT:

What shifts have I noticed since beginning to support my body's detoxification?

JOURNALING SPACE:

_____

_____

_____

Practice 6: Conscious Community

THE PRACTICE:

Cut your friend group down to a few. Limit your interactions with people who are not awakened.

This doesn't mean you become cruel or superior, it means you become intentional. You stop spending hours with people who drain you, or mock your path, or pull you back into unconscious patterns.

Keep your circle small and sacred. Quality over quantity. Depth over breadth.

WHY IT MATTERS:

You are the average of the five people you spend the most time with. This is not metaphorical, it's neurological. Your brain is constantly mirroring the people around you, syncing to their energy, and adopting their beliefs. If you're surrounded by people who are asleep, your own awakening becomes exhausting to maintain. You'll find yourself dumbing down, hiding your truth, or pretending to care about things that bore your soul. This isn't sustainable. It's not about being exclusive or judgmental, it's about protecting your energy so you can actually do the work you came here to do. Find your people because they exist. Even if it's just one or two humans who truly see you, that's enough. A small circle of awakened souls is worth more than a crowd of the unconscious.

JOURNAL PROMPT:

Who in my life supports my awakening? Who depletes it? What boundary do I need to set?

JOURNALING SPACE:

_____

_____

_____

_____

Practice 7: Celestial Awareness

THE PRACTICE:

Learn to read the stars. Pay attention to your body's energy field during certain celestial movements: full moons, new moons, eclipses, planetary retrogrades, solstices, and equinoxes.

Start simple: get a basic astronomy book or download an app on your device, and learn what's happening in the sky. Notice how you feel during major celestial events and track it in your journal.

You don't need to become an expert astrologer overnight, just start paying attention.

WHY IT MATTERS:

You are not separate from the cosmos. The same forces that move the tides move the water in your body. The same electromagnetic fields that organize stars organize your cells. Ancient peoples knew this intimately, they planted by the moon, celebrated the solstices, and tracked the constellations and wandering stars with sacred precision. Then we built cities with so much light pollution we forgot the sky existed. We started living like we're separate from the universe, and we wonder why we feel so lost. When you begin to track celestial movements and notice their effects on your energy, you remember that you are part of something vast and intelligent. You stop feeling so alone. You start to feel held by cycles bigger than your personal drama. This is not superstition; this is physics and poetry co-mingling together.

JOURNAL PROMPT:

What celestial event is happening now? What am I noticing in my body, emotions, or dreams?

JOURNALING SPACE:

_____

_____

_____

Practice 8: Listening to Earth's Messengers

THE PRACTICE:

Pay attention to the animals and plants around you. When a particular animal shows up repeatedly, in physical form, in dreams, or in conversations, notice; because that is guidance.

Learn what different animals symbolize across cultures. A hawk showing up three times in one week is not coincidence. A spider building a web on your doorstep is not random.

If you have a garden, spend time listening to your plants. Yes, listening. They communicate through growth patterns, through thriving or wilting, and through what they attract or repel.

WHY IT MATTERS:

Indigenous cultures have always known that animals are messengers and plants are teachers. Modern society called this primitive and taught us to ignore it. But you've awakened now so you know better. Everything is conscious. Everything is communicating. Animals operate on instinct, which is pure connection to source. When they show up in your life, especially repeatedly, they're bringing you information. The hawk, for instance, says, "see from a higher perspective". The snake says, "shed what no longer serves". The crow says, "magic is at work" and to "seize the opportunities as they appear". Your garden plants will tell you when they need water, when they're happy, or when the soil is depleted. You just have to slow down enough to notice. This practice develops your intuition and reminds you that you're in constant conversation with the living world.

JOURNAL PROMPT:

What animal or plant has been showing up for me? What might it be trying to communicate?

JOURNALING SPACE:

Practice 9: Grow a Garden

THE PRACTICE:

Grow a garden. Even if it's just herbs on a windowsill or one tomato plant on a balcony.

Put your hands in soil, plant seeds, water them, and watch them grow. Harvest what you've grown and eat it.

This is not optional for the awakened soul. Find a way.

WHY IT MATTERS:

There is no faster way to remember that you are part of nature's cycle than to grow your own food. You plant a seed, a tiny, seemingly dead thing, and through some miracle, it becomes a living plant that feeds and sustains you. This is pure creation. This is magic. This is the universe showing you how manifestation works. You'll learn patience because gardens don't rush. You'll learn trust because you can't control everything.

You'll learn reciprocity because you feed the soil and the soil feeds you. And you'll remember, in your body and soul, that life is constantly renewing itself. Every seed contains the memory of every plant that came before it. Every harvest promises another beginning. When you feel hopeless about the state of the world, go tend your garden. It will teach you everything you need to know about life cycles, about death and rebirth, and about faith.

JOURNAL PROMPT:

What am I growing? What is it teaching me about patience, cycles, or renewal?

JOURNALING SPACE:

_____

_____

_____

_____

Practice 10: The Temporary Nature of Physical Reality

THE PRACTICE:

Remind yourself daily that this is all temporary. You are part of the universe having a human experience, and your experience is being recorded in the Akashic records.

Be thankful that you get to simultaneously witness and experience the physical world as an aspect of the Great Spirit.

Say it out loud if you need to. Write it down. Meditate on it. Let it sink into your bones.

WHY IT MATTERS:

This is the foundation that holds all the other practices. When you truly understand that this physical life is temporary, that you are an eternal being playing in the realm of form, everything shifts. The things you were afraid of lose their power. The things you were chasing lose their urgency. Death is no longer terrifying, it's just a costume change. Failure is no longer devastating, it's just information. Other people's opinions are no longer crushing, they're just other perspectives in the great cosmic play. You stop taking everything so personally because you remember that you are not just this body, this name, this story; you are the universe experiencing itself. You are the Great Spirit dancing in form for a brief, precious moment. And every single experience whether painful, joyful, or mundane, is being recorded in the Akashic records, the infinite library of all existence. Nothing is wasted and nothing is meaningless. You are here to experience, you are here to witness, you are here to love, and you are here to create. That's it. That's the whole assignment.

JOURNAL PROMPT:

What would change in my life if I truly knew, in my bones, that this is temporary and I am eternal?

JOURNALING SPACE:

You've completed the Foundation Practices. Before you consider moving to Mastery, ask yourself: Have these become second nature? Are they fully integrated into your daily life? Can you return to them without effort or without thinking?

If yes, beautiful. Turn the page.

If not, stay here. There is no rush. The foundation is everything.

INTERLUDE: CHECKPOINT

Before You Continue: A Note on Advanced Practices

Stop here.

Seriously. Put the book down for a moment and take a breath.

If you've been working with the Foundation Practices and feel eager to move into Mastery, that eagerness itself is worth examining. Is it coming from ego's desire to be "advanced"? Or is it coming from genuine readiness?

The practices in Part Three are not more valuable than the practices in Part Two. They're not "better", they're simply different. They are more intense, more demanding, and more destabilizing if attempted before you're ready.

Mastery practices require:

- At least seven years of consistent spiritual practice (ideally fourteen to twenty-one)

- A stable foundation in the basics of grounding, nourishment, detoxification, and conscious community
- Healed major trauma (or at least active healing work with support)
- Genuine self-discipline (not the forced kind, but the kind that flows from deep commitment)
- Energetic stability (meaning you're not constantly thrown off balance by life's challenges)
- Humility (you are aware of how much you don't know)

Here's the truth about rushing:

If you try to eliminate fear before you've learned to ground yourself, you'll become untethered. If you try to control your dreams before you've cleaned up your waking life, you'll just bring chaos into your sleep. If you try to master manifestation before you've mastered discipline, you'll create from ego's desires instead of soul's purpose.

The advanced practices are potent, and they work. This is exactly why they require a stable container.

Think of it this way: The Foundation Practices build the vessel, and the Mastery Practices fill it with increasingly refined energy. If your vessel has cracks, the energy just leaks out. Or worse, it can shatter the vessel entirely.

So, before you continue, honestly assess:

Are you grounding yourself daily without having to remind yourself? Are you eating consciously? Have you simplified your social circle? Do you have a garden growing? Are you tracking celestial movements? Can you return to stillness when life gets chaotic?

If the answer is yes, if the Foundation Practices have become as natural as breathing, then you're probably ready.

If the answer is no, if you're still struggling to maintain the basics, then stay where you are. Master the foundation. In fact, there is profound wisdom in simplicity. Some of the most awakened beings who ever lived never moved beyond what we've covered in Part Two.

A warning about spiritual bypassing:

The advanced practices can become seductive to those who are not ready. They (falsely) promise power, control, and even transcendence. Be very careful here. If you're using advanced practices to avoid feeling your feelings or to escape your humanity, or to prove you're special - Stop. That is not awakening, that is just a more sophisticated form of sleep.

True mastery includes your humanity, it doesn't transcend it. You don't become less human as you awaken - you actually become more fully human, and simultaneously, more fully divine.

How will you know when you're truly ready?

You won't be asking anymore. You won't be seeking permission or validation. You'll simply know. Similar to the way you know when you're hungry or tired. It will be quiet and certain, not dramatic or urgent. And it will feel right.

And when that moment comes, the practices will be here waiting for you.

Self-Assessment Questions

Answer these honestly. Take your time. No one is watching and no one is grading you.

1. How long have I been consciously walking a spiritual path?

_____

_____

2. Which Foundation Practice still feels difficult or inconsistent for me?

_____

_____

3. What am I hoping to gain from the Mastery Practices? (Be brutally honest.)

_____

_____

4. Have I healed my major wounds, or am I hoping advanced practices will heal them for me?

_____

_____

5. Do I have a daily spiritual practice that I maintain even when I don't feel like it?

_____

_____

6. Can I sit in stillness for twenty minutes without distraction or discomfort?

_____

_____

7. Do I have at least one person in my life who can call me out when my ego is running the show?

_____

8. What scares me most about moving into advanced work?

9. If I stayed at the Foundation level for the rest of my life, would that feel like failure? Why?

10. Am I rushing because I'm genuinely ready, or because I'm uncomfortable where I am?

My Awakening Journey So Far...

Take some time here. Reflect on where you were when you first woke up, and where you are now. What has changed? What has been hard? What has surprised you? What are you grateful for?

This is your story. Honor it.

_____

_____

_____

_____

_____

_____

_____

_____

_____

If you're continuing to Part Three, welcome. You've earned this.

If you're returning to Part Two, wise choice. There is no shame in taking your time.

Either way, you're exactly where you need to be.

PART THREE: MASTERY PRACTICES

For those who have walked the path for seven years or more

A Final Word Before We Begin:

What follows is not theory. These practices have been tested in the lived experience by countless awakened beings across millennia. They work. They're also demanding, destabilizing, and will require everything you've built in your foundation.

You'll be working with the nature of reality, which are your fears, your words, your dreams, and your thoughts. You'll be asked to take complete responsibility for your experience. This means no more blaming, no more victimhood, and no more pretending you're not powerful.

This is the path of the conscious creator.

Move slowly and be patient with yourself. Remember: mastery is not about perfection; it's about devotion to the practice, even when you fail, when you forget, and when you fall back into old patterns.

The universe is infinitely forgiving. Be that forgiving with yourself.

Practice 11: Eliminating Fear

THE PRACTICE:

Eliminate fear completely and irrevocably from your consciousness.

There are only two states of being: love and fear. Everything else is a derivation of these two.

If you feel fear at any point in your day - Stop. Right there. Stop what you're doing, address the feeling then eliminate it from your consciousness. Root it out as you would an invasive weed in your garden. Every single time.

Even the fear of death. Especially the fear of death.

There is no such thing as death, therefore, there is nothing to fear.

WHY IT MATTERS:

Fear is the opposite of love, and love is your natural state. Fear is learned. Every fear you carry was taught to you by parents, by society, by trauma, and by the world's insistence that you're separate, vulnerable and mortal. But none of it is true. You are an eternal being and the worst thing that can happen to your physical body is that it stops working, and then you continue on in a different form. That's it. Everything else - rejection, failure, loss, pain - is a temporary experience and not an existential threat. When you eliminate fear, you reclaim your power. You stop making decisions from contraction and start making them from expansion. You stop living small to stay safe and start living large because you remember you can't actually be destroyed. This practice will change everything. It will take years, maybe even a lifetime to master. And that's okay. Every moment you catch fear and choose love instead; you're rewiring millennia of human conditioning.

JOURNAL PROMPT:

What fear showed up today? Where do I feel it in my body? What happens if I choose love instead?

JOURNALING SPACE:

Practice 12: The Power of Words

THE PRACTICE:

Guard your words carefully. Do not speak carelessly.

Every word you utter is a directive to the universe.

If you speak of limitation, your world will become limited. If you speak of limitless potential, your world will become limitless.

This means: Stop complaining. Stop saying "I can't." Stop joking about your failures. Stop participating in gossip. Stop agreeing when others speak negatively about themselves or the world.

Speak only what you want to create.

WHY IT MATTERS:

Words are not neutral. They're spells (notice the connection: spelling). They carry frequency, intention, and creative power. The universe doesn't distinguish between what you really mean and what you casually say.

It simply responds to the vibration you're putting out. When you say "I'm so broke," the universe hears the command: create more experience of broke-ness. When you say "I'm terrible with money," you're programming reality to give you difficulty with finances. When you say "nothing ever works out for me," you're placing an order for more disappointment. This isn't punishment. This is law. You are a creator being. Your words shape reality. Most people use this power unconsciously. They are careless with their words and destructive with their thoughts. You're awake now so you know better. Guard your words like you guard your most precious possession, because your words are creating your most precious possession: your life.

JOURNAL PROMPT:

What limiting phrase do I say habitually? What would I say instead if I believed my words create reality?

JOURNALING SPACE:

AFFIRMATIONS

The power of words extends to affirmations. These are spoken declarations that align your consciousness with divine truth. The following affirmations, adapted from the teachings of Florence Scovel Shinn and Napoleon Hill, are tools for manifesting abundance and dissolving obstacles. Speak them aloud daily, with conviction and feeling.

ABUNDANCE & PROSPERITY

- I claim my birthright of infinite abundance and prosperity.

- All that is mine by divine right is now released and reaches me in great avalanches of abundance under grace in miraculous ways.

CREATIVITY & PURPOSE

- Infinite intelligence guides me to my true work. I am compensated in wondrous ways for doing what I love.

- My imagination is where the invisible becomes visible. Through inspired thought and aligned action, I manifest my soul's vision.

INNER STRENGTH & POWER

- I transmute all obstacles into blessings. There is no force in the universe that can block my highest good.

- I am the master of my fate and the captain of my soul. No person, circumstance, or condition can limit me without my consent.

HEALTH & BALANCE

- Divine love dissolves and dissipates every wrong condition from my mind, body and affairs.
- Divine love floods my consciousness with health and every cell in my body is filled with light.

TRUSTING THE PATH

- I am in harmony with infinite intelligence and its perfect timing. All that is mine by divine right comes to me in the appointed hour.

- I walk my path with courage, knowing the universe conspires in my favor at every turn.

RELEASING FEAR & DOUBT

- I refuse to give power to fear. I stand fearless in the knowledge that I am divinely protected and guided.

- I banish doubt from my mind. I proceed with absolute certainty that infinite intelligence guides my every step.

WORTHINESS & IDENTITY

- I am not bound by the limitations that others have accepted. I claim my divine inheritance of infinite possibility.

- I am the master of my inner kingdom. No external condition can diminish the infinite power that dwells within me.

MAGNETISM & ATTRACTION

- I am a magnet for miracles. The people, resources, and opportunities I need are drawn to me effortlessly.

- My vibration attracts my tribe. I am surrounded by those who see me, support me, and celebrate my awakening.

CREATION & MANIFESTATION

- My voice is an instrument of divine creation. The universe bends to the authority of my spoken word.

- I am what I think about most. My dominant thoughts crystallize into my physical reality.

Practice 13: Meditative Action & Psychic Development

THE PRACTICE:

Calm your mind and focus your thoughts meditatively while actively doing things.

Not just during seated meditation. Do this while washing dishes, while walking, while working, and while talking to people.

Eventually, with enough practice, you will become telepathic, clairaudient, clairvoyant, and possibly even telekinetic.

This is not metaphor; it is a developmental process.

WHY IT MATTERS:

Most people's minds are chaos - in a constant stream of uncontrolled thoughts, reactions, judgments, memories, or fantasies. This mental noise drowns out the subtle signals that are always present. Signals like intuitive hints, telepathic information, and energetic reading of people and situations. When you learn to calm your mind while staying active (not just on a meditation cushion), you actually create space for these abilities to emerge naturally. They're not supernatural either, they're natural capabilities that have been buried under mental clutter. Telepathy is simply reading energy; clairaudience is hearing guidance that's always present and broadcasting; clairvoyance is simply seeing what's actually there beyond the physical; and telekinesis (if you develop it, and most won't) is simply directing energy with focused intention. These abilities develop slowly, often so subtly you don't realize it's happening, then one day you'll think of someone and they'll call. Or you'll know what someone's about to say before they say it. You'll see energy fields around people. But don't chase these abilities, let them emerge as a natural byproduct of sustained mental discipline.

JOURNAL PROMPT:

What did I notice today when I brought meditative awareness to daily activities? Any subtle perceptions?

JOURNALING SPACE:

SIGNS YOU'RE ON THE PATH

As you deepen your practice, you'll notice shifts; some will be subtle, some will be undeniable. These are signs that you're walking the path of awakening. Don't chase them, but notice them when they appear.

☐ Synchronicities occur with increasing frequency

☐ Certain animals appear repeatedly in your life (in physical form, dreams, or conversations)

☐ The right people arrive at exactly the right moment

☐ You see patterns in nature (trees, grass, wind) that feel harmonic and meaningful

☐ Your senses sharpen: hearing, sight, taste become more acute

☐ You occasionally hear the thoughts of others before they speak

☐ You experience unexplainable knowing (information that arrives without explanation)

☐ Your intuition becomes so strong you trust it implicitly

☐ Dreams become vivid, memorable, and sometimes prophetic

☐ You feel increasingly comfortable with silence and solitude

☐ Material concerns lose their grip on you

☐ You recognize teachers and lessons everywhere

☐ Time feels different (sometimes nonlinear)

☐ You feel less afraid of death

☐ Love becomes your default response, even in difficult situations

Remember: These signs are not goals. They're simply evidence that you're becoming more awake. Don't measure your worth by how many boxes you can check.

Practice 14: Dream Mastery & Astral Work

THE PRACTICE:

Record your dreams every morning until they become extremely vivid and you can recall them as clearly as memories.

Train yourself to re-enter dreams, to pick up where you left off the night before, the week before, even the year before.

Eventually, you will be able to control your dreams and decide what happens in them.

Dream Training Tips:

- When you see a mirror in a dream, look into it.
- Allow yourself to look at your hands while you're dreaming.
- Pay attention to your surroundings, do you recognize any people or places?
- Activate your senses: What do you see? What smells do you notice? What sounds are present? What is the temperature? Are

you hot or cold? Is it raining? Can you feel the rain? How cold is the snow?
- Notice when you shift into a different environment: Can you remember how you got there? Are you with the same people?
- When you come to the realization that you are in a dream, command yourself to levitate: Jump into the air and *decide* not to fall. At this point you will be able to fly. This is dream mastery.

Dream Mastery Tips:

- Focus on your destination and go there - either by dream flight (if you have traveled there in the waking state), or teleportation.
- When you are in an environment, pay attention to what you are doing.
- Continue to look at your hands to ensure you are in your own body. If you are not, focus on where you are and who you are interacting with. If you recognize a person or group of people, listen carefully.

- If you recognize a personal connection, speak with them and ask if they are aware that they are dreaming. If they are, reach out to them in the waking state to confirm the dream-share.

At dream mastery level, you can receive information from the universe, access past lives, connect to people across the world, dream-share, and remote view through people who are awake.

WHY IT MATTERS:

Dreams are not random neural transmissions. They're a doorway to consciousness beyond the physical. When you're asleep, the ego's control loosens and you have access to information you can't reach in waking life. Most people waste this opportunity. They let dreams wash over them passively, forget them by breakfast, and never realize they're standing at the threshold of infinite knowledge every single night. Dream mastery is about becoming conscious while you sleep. When you can do this, you're no longer limited by time or space. You can visit other realms. You can speak with guides, with those who are no longer in physical form, and with your higher self. You can work out problems, analyze waking situations, and receive creative downloads. You can even meet with other dreamers. This is real, as it has been documented and verified. Two people who are skilled at lucid dreaming can agree to meet in the dream space and will both remember the encounter. Alternatively, it can happen at random with someone you have a close connection to. But this is advanced work and it usually takes years for people to develop the skill. For now, start simply with recording dreams. And respect the process.

JOURNAL PROMPT:

What dream images or symbols keep recurring for me? What might they be trying to communicate?

JOURNALING SPACE:

_____

_____

_____

Practice 15: Understanding Imbalance vs. Illness

THE PRACTICE:

Recognize that there is no such thing as illness, only imbalance.

Dis-ease is just that: *not at ease*

Every skin eruption, every ache, every dis-ease is the body's natural healing and recalibration process. This occurs in plants and animals as well.

Persistent imbalance can become permanent if it is not addressed and reoriented. Or if human intervention disrupts the healing process.

Use tools such as infrared sauna, light therapy, sound bathing, hypnosis, reiki, massage, and acupuncture. Or simply ask yourself before sleep: "What is the root of this imbalance?" Once the answer is given, reframe your mind to resolve the issue.

Keep in mind: There is no such thing as contagion, only fear, which spreads to cause panic, hysteria, and confusion. It is the fear of "what is happening to them will happen to me". This is an illusion; it is only happening in your mind. Eliminate fear completely (Practice 11), and the contagion will not affect you.

And sweat. Often. Ideally once a week. If you have a particularly stressful life, schedule a sweat inducing activity two or three times a week. This is not an option. Sweating is the body's way of removing waste through the skin, waste that can cause damage or create chronic conditions if not eliminated. Night sweats occur when the body is removing bacteria and byproducts that have built up throughout the days, weeks or months. If you sweat often in your sleep, rejoice that your body's processes are working properly, however, consider adjusting your lifestyle to avoid stress overload.

WHY IT MATTERS:

Modern medicine treats the body like a broken machine: find the part that's malfunctioning and fix or remove it. But your body is not a machine. It's an intelligent, self-regulating system constantly working toward homeostasis. What we call "illness" is usually the body's attempt to heal an underlying imbalance, whether energetic, emotional, nutritional, or spiritual. A rash is not the problem, it's the body trying to expel toxins. The body's response to what GNM calls a "biological conflict". An example of this is a "separation conflict", experienced as an unwanted separation (not being able to embrace or hold a favorite person or pet). When the conflict is resolved, a rash appears to facilitate waste removal from the body. This is a natural healing process and can be observed in plants and animals as well. Another kind of "biological conflict" is an "attack conflict". Being cut with a scalpel, injections, vaccinations, stabbing or piercing pain, a physical blow against the body, or a verbal assault such as being yelled at or scolded, can all be registered as an "attack conflict". This event causes a proliferation of the skin or organ to protect against further attacks. When the conflict is resolved, this boil or compact growth (melanoma), using bacteria within the body, begins the waste removal process and ultimately disappears. Human intervention disrupts this which can cause the process to prolong, become chronic, or recur. Common cold, a dual conflict tract, and allergies, a chronic conflict tract, derive from not wanting to "swallow" a situation or accept what "stinks". Expectation or fear of an illness can cause it to occur. Inflammation is not the enemy; it's the internal system responding to a real, or perceived, threat. Pain is not a malfunction; it's information. When you understand this, you stop suppressing symptoms and start addressing root causes. You ask: What is my body trying to tell me? What balance have I lost? What do I need to change? Sometimes the answer is physical (different food, more rest). Sometimes it's emotional (unexpressed grief, unprocessed anger, fear). Sometimes it's spiritual (disconnection from purpose, misalignment with truth). Your body always knows. Your body always heals. You just have to listen.

JOURNAL PROMPT:

What physical symptom am I experiencing? What might my body be trying to communicate through it?

JOURNALING SPACE:

Practice 16: Natural Fibers & Energetic Harmony

THE PRACTICE:

Wear only cotton, linen, wool, cashmere, silk, or sustainable leather clothing.

No synthetic fabrics. No polyester, no nylon, no acrylic, no spandex.

Natural fibers only.

WHY IT MATTERS:

There is energy in natural fibers that harmonize with your skin and body. Synthetic fabrics are made from petroleum, which are liquid fossils, and they are processed into plastic threads. They don't breathe. They trap moisture and heat. They create static electricity and they disrupt your electromagnetic field. This is not woo-woo, it's measurable. Natural fibers conduct subtle energy. They allow your body to regulate its temperature naturally. They connect you to the living world (cotton from plants, wool from sheep, silk from worms, leather from plants and animals). When you wear synthetics, you're essentially wrapping yourself in plastic all day. Your skin, which is your largest organ and a major detoxification pathway, can't breathe properly and your energy field becomes distorted. You might not notice the difference immediately, but after months of wearing only natural fibers, you'll feel it; a subtle but undeniable sense of being more comfortable in your own skin, feeling more grounded and aligned.

JOURNAL PROMPT:

What synthetic items am I ready to replace? How does my body feel in natural versus synthetic clothing?

JOURNALING SPACE:

_____

_____

_____

Practice 17: Biodynamic Gardening

THE PRACTICE:

Once you are an established gardener (Practice 9), begin to sow seeds and reap your harvest with the lunar cycles.

This is called biodynamic gardening.

Get a moon calendar and follow it diligently. Learn the rhythms: The new moon is when soil is most fertile - ideal for beginning preparations, but delay sowing. The first quarter moon is the growth period - perfect for planting and sowing seeds for plants which produce above ground like tomatoes, lettuce, beans, and squash. The last quarter moon brings the lowest sap - ideal for planting root crops like carrots, beets, potatoes, as well as flowers, swedes, and grass seeds. Harvest and prune during the last quarter moon.

Work with the earth's natural rhythms, not against them.

WHY IT MATTERS:

The moon pulls the tides. The moon pulls the water in your body. The moon also pulls the water in the soil and in the sap of plants. When you plant according to lunar cycles, you're working with these forces instead of against them. Above-ground crops planted during the first quarter moon (when energy is rising) grow more vigorously. Root crops planted during the last quarter moon (when sap is pulled down into roots) develop stronger, more robust root systems. Plants harvested during the last quarter moon when sap is lower store better and maintain their vitality. Indigenous and traditional farmers have known this for thousands of years. Modern industrial agriculture ignores this because it's inconvenient for mass production. But you're not farming for profit, you're farming for connection and alignment with natural law. Biodynamic gardening is a practice in surrender. You can't rush the moon. You have to plan, wait, and coordinate with forces larger than yourself. This is good medicine for the ego. And the results speak for themselves: more vigorous plants, better harvests, and a deeper relationship with the land.

JOURNAL PROMPT:

What lunar phase are we in now? What does my garden need during this phase?

JOURNALING SPACE:

_____

_____

_____

_____

_____

_____

_____

_____

_____

_____

Practice 18: Sacred Hair Practices

THE PRACTICE:

Avoid cutting your hair off, but do trim your hair with the rhythms of the moon.

Avoid cutting your beard off, but do trim it with the rhythms of the moon.

Work with the lunar phases intentionally:

New Moon – Focus on scalp health. Detoxify, deep condition, use hair masks. This phase supports fresh starts and creating healthy foundations for growth.

First Quarter (Waxing) Moon – Nourish and strengthen. The waxing phase is fertile and wet which is ideal for hydrating treatments and supporting your hair's natural growth cycle.

Full Moon – Trim for thickness and strength. The full moon's peak energy amplifies growth. Cutting during this phase encourages stronger, more vigorous regrowth.

Last Quarter (Waning) Moon – Release and clarify. Trim split ends, remove damaged hair, cleanse away buildup. This phase supports letting go of what no longer serves.

WHY IT MATTERS:

Hair is not dead protein., it's an antenna. Every spiritual tradition that values power, intuition, and connection to the divine has specific practices around hair. Samson's strength was in his hair. Sikh warriors never cut theirs. Native American scouts kept their hair long because it sharpened their senses. Hindu sadhus grow their locks for decades. There's wisdom here that science is only beginning to measure: that hair functions as an extension of the nervous system, picking up subtle environmental information. At minimum, hair follicles are connected to your nervous system and your endocrine system. When you cut your hair significantly, you're severing these connections. Many people report feeling disoriented, less intuitive, more anxious after major haircuts. If you've been cutting your hair short your whole life, you won't know what you're missing. Let it grow. Tend to it as you tend to your garden. Trim it according to natural rhythms. See what you notice.

JOURNAL PROMPT:

What is my relationship with my hair? What would change if I saw it as sacred rather than cosmetic?

JOURNALING SPACE:

_____

_____

_____

_____

_____

_____

_____

_____

Practice 19: Lunar Cycle Syncing (For Women)

THE PRACTICE:

If you are a woman, pre-menopause, your monthly cycle should be synced to the moon by now.

If not, detox your body. Become vegetarian or fast for several days at a time until you are synced.

Your body knows how to do this. You just need to remove the interference.

WHY IT MATTERS:

For thousands of years, women's bodies naturally cycled with the moon, either menstruating with the new moon, ovulating with the full moon, or vice versa depending on whether they were in their "mother phase" or "wise woman phase." This synchronization is not coincidence as both cycles are approximately 28-29 days. Both are responding to the same gravitational and electromagnetic rhythms. Modern life has disrupted this: artificial light at night, hormonal birth control, environmental toxins, processed foods, stress, etc. When your cycle is synced with the moon, you're in harmony with one of the largest rhythmic forces affecting the earth. You'll notice your intuition heightens during certain phases. Your energy naturally waxes and wanes in predictable patterns. You can plan your life accordingly, knowing when you'll be outward-focused and when you'll need to turn inward. This is your birthright as a woman. Reclaim it. The moon is calling you home.

JOURNAL PROMPT:

Where am I in my cycle? Where is the moon in its' cycle? What needs to shift for these to align?

JOURNALING SPACE:

_____

_____

_____

Practice 20: Visualization & Manifestation

THE PRACTICE:

Visualize every outcome before it happens. Only visualize what you desire.

See it in vivid detail; not just the end result, but the feeling of it, the texture, the sounds, the conversations, and the sensations in your body.

Remember: your thoughts shape your reality. You will always receive what you ask for, though it may not show up in the way you expect.

WHY IT MATTERS:

Consciousness creates reality. Not eventually, constantly. Every thought is a blueprint. Every emotion is a magnetic charge. Every visualization is a prototype. The universe doesn't respond to what you say you want; it responds to the vibration you're emitting. When you visualize something with enough clarity, emotion, and repetition, you're not just imagining, you're building it in the energetic realm first. Then physical reality has no choice but to conform. This is how every great achievement begins: as a vision in someone's mind that they held so consistently it had to materialize. But here's the key: you can't visualize from fear or lack. You can't imagine your desired outcome while simultaneously believing it's impossible. The visualization must be paired with the felt sense of already having it. This is why mastery requires eliminating fear first (Practice 11). When fear is gone, visualization becomes pure creation.

JOURNAL PROMPT:

What am I calling into my life? Can I feel it as if it's already here?

JOURNALING SPACE:

_____

_____

Practice 21: Karma – Cause & Effect

THE PRACTICE:

Know the fundamentals of cause and effect.

Every action creates a reaction. Every thought creates a ripple. Every choice creates a consequence.

Nothing is random. Nothing is punishment. Everything is feedback.

Study karma, not as a punitive system, but as natural law; such as thermodynamics or the conservation of energy.

WHY IT MATTERS:

Karma is not the universe keeping score and punishing you for bad behavior. Karma is simply the law of cause and effect playing out across time and space. When you understand this deeply, you stop being a victim. You realize that everything in your life is either a direct result of your past actions, thoughts, and choices, or it's an opportunity to respond in a new way and create different karma going forward. This is radically empowering and radically humbling at the same time. It means you're responsible. YOU ARE RESPONSIBLE. No one is doing this to you. You're not cursed. You're not unlucky. You are, in fact, experiencing the natural consequences of energies you set in motion, either in this life, or in previous ones. And the beautiful thing about understanding karma is that once you see the pattern, you can change it. Different actions, different thoughts, different choices = different karma = different life. You are not doomed to repeat the past. You have complete agency in every moment to shift the trajectory of your own life.

JOURNAL PROMPT:

What pattern keeps repeating in my life? What might I be doing to perpetuate it?

JOURNALING SPACE:

Practice 22: Sacred Languages

THE PRACTICE:

Learn Egyptian, Hebrew, Sanskrit, and any Roman/Latin-based language.

Most old texts are written in these languages and each unlocks a different dimension of spiritual truth.

Egyptian preserves the original phonetic sounds and pure creative concepts at the foundation of all language. These hieroglyphs encode the primordial vibrations of creation itself, revealing how sound and symbol birth meaning into existence.

Hebrew is an alphanumeric language where every letter carries a numerical value, creating layers of coded meaning. Built upon Egyptian phonetic foundations, Hebrew encodes the original sacred sounds within its structure, while adding mathematical relationships that reveal hidden spiritual connections. Words with the same numerical sum are considered spiritually related, creating webs of divine mathematics woven throughout sacred texts.

Romance languages (French, Spanish, Italian, Portuguese, Romanian) trace the evolution of spiritual vocabulary across Western culture. By understanding how concepts transformed as they moved through time and geography, you can see what was preserved, what shifted, and what was reinterpreted.

Latin reveals how mystical concepts became hidden in metaphor and allegory as Christianity moved away from its esoteric roots. Understanding Latin exposes what was deliberately veiled, allowing you to decode the symbolic language that conceals deeper truths.

Sanskrit is both a vibrational and philosophical language. The sounds themselves are considered sacred, and single words contain multiple dimensions of meaning invisible in translation.

WHY IT MATTERS:

Translation always loses something. When sacred texts are translated into English, layers of meaning disappear – sometimes accidentally, sometimes deliberately. These five language families represent different stages in humanity's spiritual evolution and different ways of encoding truth. Egyptian came first, carrying the pure creative sounds and archetypal concepts. Hebrew encoded these truths in sacred mathematics and alphanumeric relationships. Sanskrit developed in the East, preserving vibrational power and multi-layered philosophy. Latin and Romance languages show how Western civilization fragmented and transformed (or concealed) these original teachings as they spread across cultures throughout the centuries. Understanding even basic concepts in these languages transforms how you reach ancient wisdom. For example, in Egyptian:

Maat – Truth, justice, harmony, balance, order, and cosmic law. Maat is a concept representing the fundamental order of the universe. Divine law.

Ba – The soul or spiritual essence, often depicted as a human-headed bird. The Ba represents your personality, individual characteristics, and unique spiritual identity that can travel between physical and spiritual realms. This is the eternal part of you that continues after death.

Ra – Represents life-giving power, creation, light, and divine kingship. Ra, depicted as the sun, journeys daily across the sky and through the underworld, symbolizing the eternal cycle of death and rebirth. A teaching encoded in countless myths.

Ptah – The creator which brought the world into being through thought and speech. Ptah conceived creation through the mind and manifested it through words. This is the divine embodiment of conscious creation – the same principle you're working with in Practice 12 (The Power of Words) and Practice 20 (Visualization & Manifestation).

When all of these concepts are combined, they form the phrase: **MAAT-BA-RA-PTAH** or simply, **MAHABHARATA**.

Mahabharata is the sacred Hindu text that explores dharma (cosmic duty), and karma (Practice 21) through epic poetry. Single Sanskrit words often contain entire philosophical concepts which can be traced to the origin of phonetical language.

This is not quick work. Learning languages takes years. But for someone committed to deep study of sacred texts (Practice 1 and Practice 23), it's essential.

JOURNAL PROMPT:

What sacred text do I want to understand more deeply?
What language would unlock it for me?

JOURNALING SPACE:

_____

_____

_____

_____

_____

_____

_____

_____

_____

Practice 23: Astrological Wisdom in Ancient Texts

THE PRACTICE:

Study advanced astrological movements and cycles, then re-read every sacred text from every ancient culture (Practice 1).

Focus on understanding:

Precession of the equinoxes – the slow wobble of the zodiac over approximately 26,000 years, creating the framework for understanding "ages" (Age of Aquarius, Age of Pisces, etc.)

Retrogrades – the apparent backward motion of the wandering stars from Earth's perspective, which ancient texts use to symbolize periods of inward reflection, revision and karmic reckoning.

Houses – the twelve divisions of the sky representing different life areas (self, resources, communication, home, creativity, health, partnerships, transformation, wisdom, career, community, and spirituality)

Aspects – the angular relationships between celestial bodies (conjunctions, oppositions, trines, and squares) that create harmonious or challenging energies in both the heavens and human experience.

Transits – the ongoing movement of wandering stars through the zodiac and how their positions activate different themes, energies, and collective experiences throughout time.

The sacred texts are referring to the movements and cycles of the natural world and rarely (if ever) literal people or places. For example:

Jesus is not a person. Jesus represents the astrological time period of Pisces, depicted as two fish. An approximately ~2,100-year cycle, Pisces was a time period of faith, religion, organized belief systems, hierarchy, illusions and deception.

Bal is not a person. Bal represents the astrological time period of Taurus, depicted as the bull. An approximately ~2,100-year cycle, Taurus was a time period of sense exploration of the physical world, stability, agriculture, and monumental infrastructure.

Moses is not a person. Moses represents the astrological time period of Aries, depicted as the ram's horn. A time when people were able to "draw knowledge from" or were "born of" the Great Spirit. Eras of Moses include the time periods of:

Thutmose – drawing knowledge from Thoth (thought)

Rameses – drawing knowledge from Ra (the sun or energetic principle of the sun)

Remember, the phonetic structure of words (Practice 22) can be reflected across astrology, languages and cultures: Jesus = Yeshua = Joshua. Christ = Krist = Krishna. Bal = Bull = Bell. Moses = Mese = Mexi = Mexican = Mohican.

WHY IT MATTERS:

This will completely transform how you read scripture. When you understand that ancient texts are encoded with astronomical information, suddenly the "stories" reveal themselves as star maps, as descriptions of celestial mechanics, as teaching tools for understanding cosmic cycles. The twelve disciples are the twelve signs of the zodiac. Christ is crucified on the cross at the winter solstice when the sun "dies" or appears to cease movement in the skies. This is not diminishing these texts; it's revealing their sophistication. Ancient peoples embedded multiple layers of meaning into their stories. Moral teachings, historical records, AND astronomical data. They knew the heavens intimately because their survival depended on it, and they understood that "as above, so below". They understood that celestial patterns mirror and influence earthly experience. When you learn to read texts as astronomy, and interpret its wisdom into your own life, you gain access to knowledge that has been hidden in plain sight for thousands of years. You begin to see how solar and lunar cycles, planetary movements, and the precession of the equinoxes are encoded in mythology, religious calendars, and prophecy.

JOURNAL PROMPT:

What sacred text passage have I read many times? What might it mean if it's describing celestial movements?

JOURNALING SPACE:

Practice 24: Discipline & Integrity

THE PRACTICE:

Keep your word. Be disciplined in everything that you do.

If you say you'll do something, do it. If you can't do it, don't say you will.

Let your yes be yes and your no be no.

Apply this same discipline to your practices, your health, your relationships, and your creative work.

WHY IT MATTERS:

Integrity is the foundation of all power. Not power over others but power to create, to manifest, and to align with your highest self. Every time you break your word (to yourself or to others), you fracture your integrity. You train yourself to not trust yourself. You scatter your energy. You become unreliable to the universe. Why would the universe deliver on your intentions if you don't follow through on your own commitments? Discipline is not punishment. It's devotion. It's saying: this matters enough that I'll show up even when I don't feel like it. Even when it's hard. Even when no one's watching. The practices in this book only work if you do them consistently. Not perfectly, but persistently. Mastery is not talent, it's not intelligence, and it's not luck. It's showing up, again and again, whether you feel inspired or not. When you develop true discipline, you become truly unshakeable. Life can throw chaos at you, and you'll stay steady because you've trained yourself to keep showing up for what matters.

JOURNAL PROMPT:

Where have I been breaking my word to myself or others? What would change if I kept it?

JOURNALING SPACE:

_____

_____

_____

Practice 25: You Are the Creator

THE PRACTICE:

Remember: You are the creator of your reality.

No one can change anything in your life that you did not consent to, consciously or unconsciously.

Everyone and every circumstance that shows up is here to help you on the path that you, consciously or unconsciously, wish to create.

All creation is a manifestation of the Great Spirit.

WHY IT MATTERS:

This is the ultimate teaching. The final practice. The one that contains all the others.

You are not a victim of your circumstances. You are not at the mercy of other people's choices. You are not a leaf blown by the wind. You are the wind. You are the tree. You are the entire forest.

Every person in your life, difficult or delightful, is there because some part of you called them in. Every obstacle you face is an obstacle you chose (even if unconsciously) because you needed to learn something, heal something, or become something. Every blessing is evidence of alignment. Every challenge is an invitation to grow.

This is not blame. This is total empowerment.

When you truly understand that you are the creator, you stop waiting for someone to save you. You stop blaming your parents, your ex, your boss, the government, the economy, etc. Not because they're blameless, but because their power over you is only as strong as you allow it to be.

You are an expression of the Great Spirit – the same force that creates stars and grows flowers and beats your heart without your conscious effort. That force is creating through you, as you, right now.

The question is: are you creating consciously or unconsciously?

Mastery is learning to create consciously.

It's learning to choose your thoughts deliberately, to speak your reality into being intentionally, to visualize your path clearly, and to take full responsibility of your life.

This is the work. This is the path. This is what you came here to do.

You are the creator of your reality.

Act like it.

JOURNAL PROMPT:

What am I creating right now with my thoughts, words, and actions? Is this what I truly want?

JOURNALING SPACE:

_____

_____

_____

_____

_____

_____

_____

_____

_____

_____

_____

_____

You've completed the Mastery Practices.

But the work is never complete. These practices are not a checklist, they're a way of life.

Return to them daily. Refine them constantly. Let them evolve as you evolve.

And remember: You are not walking this path to become something you're not.

You're walking this path to remember what you've always been.

PART FOUR: INTEGRATION

Living as an Awakened Being

You've done the work. You've learned the practices. You've begun the journey of remembering who you truly are.

Now what?

Now you live it.

Integration is where the real challenge begins. Not on the meditation cushion or in the garden or in the pages of this book, but out there, in the messy, chaotic, beautiful world where most people are still asleep.

Living as an awakened being means:

Staying grounded when everyone around you is spinning. You'll be in rooms full of people arguing about things that don't matter, chasing things that won't fulfill them, or afraid of things that aren't real. Your job is not to fix them or judge them or prove you're right. Your job is to stay centered in your own knowing while remaining compassionate toward their journey.

Being in the world but not of it. You continue to pay your bills, do your work, and maintain relationships, but you're no longer fooled by the game. You participate without attachment. And you engage without losing yourself. This is a delicate balance. If you are too detached, you become ineffective; if you are too absorbed you will forget what you know.

Becoming a living example, not a preacher. People don't wake up because you lecture them about sacred geometry or tell them they're creating their reality. They wake up when they see you living differently – calmer, clearer, more aligned – and something in them recognizes it as possible. Your vibration is your message. Your peace is your sermon.

Holding space for others' awakening without forcing it. You can't wake someone up. You can only hold the door open and let them choose to walk through when they're ready. Some people you love will never wake up in this lifetime, and that's okay. Your job is to love them anyway, to honor their path, and to trust their timing.

Maintaining your practices even when life gets hard. Especially when life gets hard. The practices aren't meant for perfect conditions; they're meant for chaos, for grief, for confusion, or for those moments when you forget everything you know and feel completely lost. That's when you return to the basics: bare feet on the earth, intentional breath in your body, living food that nourishes and heals, silence that restores and recalibrates. The foundation supports you when nothing else does.

Forgiving yourself when you slip. Because you will slip. You'll react from fear instead of love. You'll speak carelessly. You'll forget to ground yourself and wonder why you feel anxious. You'll eat junk food and skip your practices and lose your center completely. This is not failure; this is being human. The awakened path includes all of it. What matters most is that you notice, course-correct then begin again.

Trusting the timing of your unfolding. Some practices will click immediately, others will take years to understand. Some teachings will land in your twenties while others won't make sense until you're sixty. The path is not linear. You'll spiral back to the same lessons at deeper levels. You'll think you've mastered something and then discover a whole new layer beneath it. This is not regression; this is how consciousness evolves. Trust the spiral nature of awakening.

Remember: Integration is not a phase you complete and move past. Integration is the rest of your life. Every day, you'll be choosing, consciously or unconsciously, whether to live from your awakened knowing or slip back into the matrix. Both options are always available and the choice is always yours.

The practices in this book are tools but you are the craftsperson. The life you build with these tools is your masterpiece.

When You Forget (And You Will)

There will be days when you forget everything.

Days when you wake up anxious, reactive, or completely disconnected from your knowing. Days when you eat junk food, snap at people you love, or spend hours scrolling mindlessly. Days when the practices feel like a burden instead of a gift, or when the whole spiritual path feels like a delusion you invented to cope with a meaningless existence.

This is normal.

This is not failure.

This is the human experience.

Here's what to do when you forget:

Don't spiral into shame. Shame is the ego's favorite trap. It will tell you that you're not spiritual enough, not disciplined enough, not awakened enough. It will compare you to some imaginary, perfected version of yourself. Don't believe it. Even the most awakened beings have hard days. Even masters forget sometimes. Your worth is not determined by your consistency.

Return to the simplest practice. You don't need to do all 25 practices perfectly to be okay. Just do one. Put your bare feet on the earth. Eat a piece of fruit. Take three deep breaths. Read one page of a sacred text. One small action reconnects you to the current. That's all you need to start flowing again.

Ask for help. From the universe, from your guides, from a trusted friend, or from your higher self. Say out loud: "I've lost my way. Help me remember." Then pay attention. Help always comes. Sometimes it's a conversation. Sometimes it's a song on the radio. Sometimes it's just a subtle shift in your energy that calms your nervous system.

Remember that forgetting is part of the design. You incarnated into a human body with a human brain that is designed to forget. The veil of forgetting is not punishment, it's actually the game. The whole point is to remember, then forget, then remember again. Each time you remember, you remember more deeply. Each time you forget, you learn what pulls you off course. This oscillation is not a bug, it's a design feature.

Be gentle with yourself. Talk to yourself the way you'd talk to a beloved friend who's struggling. You wouldn't berate them for being imperfect. You wouldn't tell them they're failing at spirituality. You'd remind them of their inherent worth. You'd tell them it's okay to rest. You'd hold space for their humanity with tenderness. Do this for yourself.

Trust that you'll return. You always do. Every time you've forgotten before, you've found your way back. You're reading this book because some part of you always returns to the path, no matter how far you wander. That part of you that keeps choosing consciousness is stronger than the part that forgets. Trust it.

The awakened path is not about never falling. It's about knowing how to get back up.

And you do. You always do.

EMERGENCY GROUNDING TECHNIQUES

When you feel ungrounded, anxious, scattered, or disconnected, use these. No explanation needed. Just do one. Immediately.

PHYSICAL GROUNDING

- Stand on bare earth (grass, soil, sand) for 5 minutes
- Touch a tree (press your palms and forehead against the trunk)
- Pet an animal (let them calm you)
- Lie flat on the ground (let the earth hold you)

BREATHWORK

- 4-7-8 breath: Inhale 4 counts, hold 7 counts, exhale 8 counts (repeat 4 times)
- Box breathing: Inhale 4, hold 4, exhale 4, hold 4 (repeat until calm)

- Bellows breath: Fast, forceful nose breathing for 30 seconds

SENSORY RESET

- Look at the sky: especially the clouds, stars, or the moon
- Listen to water: ocean, rain, a running faucet
- Listen to singing bowls, binaural beats, chimes
- Smell something strong: coffee, citrus, sage, palo santo
- Taste something intentional: dark chocolate, mint, salt

MOVEMENT

- Walk through nature with no phone or devices
- Dance any way your body wants to move
- Shake your whole body for 2 minutes
- Stretch your spine, neck, hips

PAUSE PRACTICE

- Stop whatever you're doing
- Place hand on heart
- Say out loud: "I am here. I am safe. I am held."
- Take three deep breaths

GRATITUDE PRACTICE

- Name three things that you are grateful for
- List five tings that went right today
- Think of one person you love and send them silent gratitude
- Say out loud: "I am grateful for my life and the universe that supports it."

Keep this page bookmarked. Return to it often.

Resources & Further Study

The 25 practices in this book are a starting point, not a finish line. There is always more to learn, deeper to go, and further to explore.

If you want to go deeper:

Sacred Texts: The Bhagavad Gita, Tao Te Ching, Kybalion, Egyptian Book of the Dead, Vedas and Upanishads, I Ching, Emerald Tablet of Hermes. Read them slowly. Read them multiple times. Let them unfold over years.

Astrology: Study beyond your sun sign. Learn about houses, aspects, transits, progressed charts. Understand the precession of the equinoxes. Find teachers who approach astrology as astronomy, not entertainment.

Biodynamic Practices: Research Rudolf Steiner's work on biodynamic agriculture. Learn about planting by moon signs (not just phases). Study permaculture and regenerative growing methods.

Energy and Body Work: Explore reiki, acupuncture, light therapy, sound healing, breathwork, qi gong, Chinese Medicine, Ayurveda, German New Medicine (GNM). Find practitioners who understand that these are not alternative medicine, they're primary medicine that addresses root causes.

Dream Work: Read about lucid dreaming, astral projection, remote viewing. Keep a dream journal for years, not weeks. Find communities of serious practitioners, not just hobbyists.

Sacred Languages: Take actual classes. Hebrew from qualified teachers. Egyptian through learning hieroglyphs and concepts. Latin through etymology study. Sanskrit through yoga philosophy programs. These languages unlock texts in ways that apps and YouTube videos cannot.

Community: Seek out people who are further along the path than you. Find teachers, mentors, and elders who can call you higher. Listen to your furry companions. But also stay humble enough to learn from beginners because they often see things you've forgotten.

Your Own Guidance: Ultimately, your highest teacher is within. The practices in this book are meant to strengthen your connection to that inner knowing. Trust what you receive in meditation, in dreams, or in sudden knowing. Your soul knows your path better than any book ever will.

A note on teachers and teachings:

Be discerning. Just because someone is popular, charismatic, or claims to be enlightened doesn't mean they're aligned with truth. Watch how they live, not just what they say. Do they embody integrity? Humility? Discipline? Do they keep their word? Do they empower you or do they create dependency? Trust your intuition more than their credentials.

And remember: even the best teachers are human. Take what resonates, leave what doesn't, and never give away your sovereignty to anyone, no matter how awakened they seem.

You are your own guru.

My Commitment to Consciousness

This is your declaration. Write it as if it's a contract with your soul. What are you committing to? What practices will you maintain? What old patterns are you releasing? What new way of being are you claiming?

Be specific. Be honest. Be bold.

Date it. Sign it. Return to it when you forget.

_____

_____

_____

_____

_____

_____

_____

_____

_____

_____

_____

_____

_____

_____

_____

_____

_____

_____

_____

Signature: _____

Date: _____

You've reached the end of this book.

But this is not an ending, it's a beginning.

Everything you need is already inside you.

These practices simply help you remember.

Walk gently. Walk intentionally. Walk with love.

You are not alone on this path.

You never were.

GLOSSARY

Akashic Records: The energetic archive of every thought, word, action, and experience that has ever occurred. Often described as the "universe's library" or "cosmic database," the Akashic Records contain the complete history of every soul's journey across all lifetimes. Advanced practitioners can learn to access these records through deep meditation or altered states of consciousness.

Astral Projection: The practice of consciously separating your consciousness from your physical body to travel in non-physical realms. Also called "out-of-body experience" (OBE). This is different from lucid dreaming, though the two can overlap. Advanced practitioners report visiting distant physical locations, connecting with other beings, and exploring non-physical dimensions.

Ayurveda: An ancient holistic healing system from India that views health as balance between body, mind, and spirit. Ayurveda recognizes three fundamental energies or doshas (Vata, Pitta, Kapha) that govern physical and mental processes. Ayurveda emphasizes prevention, personalized medicine, and the connection between individual health and cosmic rhythms.

Ba: In ancient Egyptian, the Ba is the soul or spiritual essence of a person, often depicted as a human-headed bird. The Ba represents your personality, individual characteristics, and unique spiritual identity that can travel between the physical and spiritual realms. It is the eternal part of you that continues after physical death.

Biodynamic Gardening: An approach to agriculture that works in harmony with lunar and cosmic rhythms, developed by Rudolf Steiner. Biodynamic farmers plant, cultivate, and harvest according to moon phases and astrological cycles, treating the farm as a living organism in relationship with celestial forces.

Binaural Beats: Audio recordings that play slightly different frequencies in each ear, causing the brain to perceive a third "beat" frequency. This phenomenon can guide the brain into specific states of consciousness (relaxation, focus, meditation, sleep) by synchronizing brainwave patterns to the perceived beat frequency.

Chinese Medicine: A comprehensive healing system based on the flow of vital life energy (Qi) through pathways in the body called meridians. Health is harmony between opposing forces (Yin and Yang) and the five elements (Wood, Fire, Earth, Metal, Water). Illness occurs when Qi becomes blocked, deficient, or excessive. Treatment includes acupuncture, herbal medicine, dietary therapy, Qigong and massage.

Clairaudience: The psychic ability to hear sounds, voices, or information beyond the normal range of hearing. This can include hearing guidance from spiritual sources or information from non-physical realms. Clairaudience is one of several psychic senses that can develop through sustained spiritual practice.

Clairvoyance: The psychic ability to see beyond normal physical sight. This can include seeing energy fields (auras), spirits, future or past events, or receiving visual information about distant locations or situations. Literally means "clear seeing."

Dharma: A Sanskrit concept with multiple interconnected meanings: cosmic law, natural order, duty, righteousness, and the path of right living. In Hindu and Buddhist traditions, following your dharma means living in alignment with your soul's purpose and the universal order.

Earth Plane: The physical, material dimension of existence where we currently live, in human bodies. The earth plane is one of many planes or dimensions of reality. It is characterized by density, time, space, and the illusion of separation. Souls incarnate on the earth plane to have experiences and learn lessons that can only be learned through physical embodiment.

German New Medicine (GNM): A medical system developed by Dr. Ryke Geerd Hamer based on Five Biological Laws that view disease as meaningful "Biological Special Programs" created by nature for survival. According to GNM, symptoms arise from specific psychological conflicts or shocks that affect both the psyche and corresponding organs simultaneously, and healing follows a predictable two-phase pattern once the conflict is resolved. GNM recognizes that what conventional medicine calls "illness" is often the body's natural healing process. Each disease corresponds to a specific type of emotional or psychological conflict (such as separation, territory loss, or fear), and symptoms appear in precise correlation with brain relays that can be seen in CT scans. Understanding the biological purpose behind symptoms allows for conscious participation in the healing process rather than fear-based intervention.

Great Spirit: A term used across many indigenous traditions to refer to the divine source, the ultimate creative force, or God. In the context of this book, Great Spirit represents the unified consciousness from which all existence emerges, it is the universe experiencing itself through infinite forms.

Karma: The law of cause and effect operating across all dimensions of existence. Every action, thought, and intention creates energy that eventually returns to its source. Karma is not punishment, its natural feedback designed to teach and balance. Understanding karma means taking complete responsibility for your experience and recognizing that you are constantly creating your future through your present choices.

Lucid Dreaming: The state of being consciously aware that you are dreaming while still in the dream. In lucid dreams, you can control the dream environment, interact intentionally with dream characters, and use the dream space for learning, healing, or spiritual exploration.

Maat: The ancient Egyptian principle of truth, justice, harmony, balance, order, and cosmic law. Maat represents the natural order of the universe. Living in accordance with Maat means living truthfully, justly, and in balance with natural and divine law.

Manifestation: The process of bringing something from the non-physical realm of thought and energy into physical reality. Based on the principle that consciousness creates reality, manifestation involves using focused intention, emotion, visualization, and aligned action to create desired outcomes.

Maya: A Sanskrit term with profound meanings across Indian philosophies. In Vedic and Hindu traditions, maya refers to the cosmic creative force through which the phenomenal world is manifested. Maya is often translated as "illusion" or "magic." It is the veil that makes the ever-changing, temporary phenomenal universe seem real and permanent, thereby concealing spiritual reality and causing us to mistake appearances for ultimate truth.

Matrix: A term popularized by the film of the same name, referring to the constructed reality of societal conditioning, beliefs, and systems that keep people unconscious and compliant. "Waking up from the matrix" means recognizing that much of what we've been taught about reality, success, and how to live is designed to maintain control rather than support genuine freedom and awakening.

Precession of the Equinoxes: The slow wobble of the heavens that causes the position of the equinoxes to shift backward through the zodiac constellations over approximately 26,000 years. This cycle is divided into twelve ages (Age of Aquarius, Age of Pisces, etc.), each lasting about 2,160 years. Ancient cultures encoded this astronomical knowledge into their sacred texts and architecture.

Ptah: The ancient Egyptian patron of craftsmen, architects, and artists. Ptah was believed to have created the world through thought and speech.

Ptah conceived of creation in mind and brought it into being through words. This makes Ptah the divine embodiment of the creative word and conscious manifestation.

Qigong: An ancient Chinese practice that combines gentle movement, breath control, meditation, and focused intention to cultivate and balance Qi (vital energy) in the body. Qigong can be practiced in stillness or motion, and is considered both a healing art and a spiritual discipline.

Ra: The ancient Egyptian sun "god". Ra represented the sun's life-giving power, creation, light, and divine kingship. Ra was depicted traveling across the sky during the day and through the underworld at night, symbolizing the eternal cycle of death and rebirth.

Reiki: A Japanese energy healing practice that channels universal life force energy through the practitioner's hands to promote healing, balance, and well-being. Reiki works on the principle that energy blockages in the body create imbalance and illness, and that flowing energy through these blockages restores health.

Remote Viewing: The practice of perceiving information about distant or unseen locations, objects, or events through psychic means. Originally developed and studied by military intelligence programs, remote viewing demonstrates that consciousness is not limited by physical distance or barriers.

Sanskrit: The ancient sacred language of India, used in Hindu and Buddhist texts including the Vedas, Upanishads, Bhagavad Gita, and Mahabharata. Sanskrit is considered a "vibrational language" where the sound of the words themselves carries spiritual power and meaning. Single Sanskrit terms often contain complex philosophical concepts that require paragraphs to explain in other languages.

Source Energy: Another term for the divine, God, universal consciousness, or the unified field from which all existence emerges. Source energy is the fundamental creative force that animates all life and maintains the universe. We are not separate from source; we are individualized expressions of it.

Spiritual Bypassing: A term coined by psychologist John Welwood to describe the use of spiritual practices and beliefs to avoid dealing with painful feelings, unresolved wounds, and developmental needs. Examples include using meditation to avoid grief, using "positive thinking" to deny legitimate anger, or claiming "everything happens for a reason" to bypass accountability. True spiritual practice includes our humanity rather than transcending it.

Telekinesis: The ability to move or influence physical objects using only mental intention, without physical contact. Also called psychokinesis. This is one of the rarest psychic abilities and typically only develops after years or decades of sustained consciousness work, if at all.

Telepathy: Direct mind-to-mind communication without using physical senses or conventional communication methods. Telepathy can manifest as suddenly knowing what someone is thinking, receiving information from distant people, or communicating with animals or plants. This ability often develops naturally as mental discipline increases.

Vibrational Frequency: Everything in existence vibrates at specific frequencies, from physical matter to thoughts and emotions. Higher vibrational frequencies (love, joy, peace, gratitude) align us with well-being and flow. Lower frequencies (fear, anger, shame, guilt) create density and resistance. Spiritual practices are designed to raise and stabilize your vibrational frequency.

Wandering Stars: The ancient term for planets. Unlike the "fixed stars" (constellations) which maintain their positions relative to each other, wandering stars appear to wander across the night sky, following their own paths through the zodiac. Ancient astronomers tracked these wandering stars meticulously, recognizing their influence on earthly events and human consciousness. Understanding the movements of wandering stars is essential to interpreting sacred texts, which often encode planetary cycles in their stories.

This glossary provides foundational definitions. As you deepen your practice and study, many of these concepts will reveal additional layers of meaning.

ABOUT THE AUTHOR

Nicole I. Burgess is an entrepreneur, actress, and spiritual seeker based in Chapel Hill, North Carolina. She graduated from Meredith College in 2012 with a BA in French and has built a diverse creative career in film, theater, publishing, and philanthropy.
As the founder of NBM Publishing, Nicole produces films, documentaries, plays, podcasts, books, and magazines. Her writing is characterized by philosophical depth, intricate character development, and vivid storytelling that invites readers and audiences into transformative journeys.

The Awakened Soul's Field Manual emerges from Nicole's own decades-long journey of spiritual practice, study of ancient wisdom traditions, and integration of consciousness work into everyday life. She writes not as a guru, but as a fellow traveler on the path, sharing what she has learned, what has worked, and what continues to unfold.

Nicole lives in Chapel Hill with her gardens, her journals, and a deep commitment to living in alignment with natural and divine law. She believes that awakening is not an escape from the world, but a return to a more present and purposeful life.

www.ingramcontent.com/pod-product-compliance
Lightning Source LLC
LaVergne TN
LVHW091538070526
838199LV00002B/111